Endorsements

Back to Love & Beauty - A collection of 16 magical notes of passion, inspiration, tenderness and warmth to my heart. This beautiful work of art will take your soul on an epic journey of rediscovery and grace. This is the perfect volume to curl up with on a cloudy day together with your favourite cup of tea and a soft blanket. Be a friend and share a copy with your dearest loved ones - their spirit and essence will most surely thank you!

—Katerina Cozias,
Hollywood-based media
& television personality

Back to Love & Beauty is a masterful blend of poetry and art that captures the essence of the human experience. Mouna's insights on love and spirituality are profound and thought-provoking, and her words will resonate with readers of all ages.

—Joe Vitale,
Bestselling Author and
Featured Teacher from *The Secret*

Mouna Saquaque has taken the reader on an irresistibly addictive tour to the deepest part of what it means to love another human. *Back to Love & Beauty's* sixteen poems and illustrations light up my imagination and remind me to remember every day to love again. Bravo, Mouna!

—Sandy Gallagher, CEO,
Proctor Gallagher Institute

It was easy to relate to Mouna Saqauque's poems. They explore the many nuances of relationships, the roles we fall into, our emotional beliefs, our power to overcome adversity, connecting with nature, seeking and finding fulfillment in life, and the chance to look at life through a different lens.

—Peggy McColl,
New York Times bestselling author

I fell in love with Mouna Saquaque's entrancing poems with their rhythm, imagery, and subtle understated style. You get a deeper meaning each time you re-read them.

—Judy O'Beirn,
International bestselling author

Back to Love & Beauty

POEMS AND ILLUSTRATIONS BY

Mouna Saquaque

Hasmark
PUBLISHING
INTERNATIONAL

Published by
Hasmark Publishing International
www.hasmarkpublishing.com

Disclaimer

Permission should be addressed in writing to Mouna Saquaque at saquaque.mouna@gmail.com

Editor: Jamie Geidel jamie@hasmarkpublishing.com
Cover Designer: Anne Karklins anne@hasmarkpublishing.com
Layout Artist: Amit Dey amit@hasmarkpublishing.com

ISBN 13: 978-1-77482-200-5
ISBN 10: 1774822008

Dedication

To my superhero, to my friend.

May you rest in peace.

Table of Contents

If I had to personify good company,
Then these poems would be my sanctuary
In moments when rationality needs beauty.
Those times, art expressions, take you there instantly.
With all my expression of Love.

I Could Have Wanted You to Stay

I could have wanted you to stay.
A timeline, where things went wrong, in the play.
We've already been separated, by distance.
But this time, I should have noticed a difference.

I think you showed me, subliminal:
No One is yours, or eternal.
It's not about you, nothing personal.
This is how life is, unfolding normal.

I got used to you, my hero, my friend.
Our relationship is far from an End.
You crossed the veil, reached the magical Covenant
I see you through the blinds, smiling, content.

You can only tell a story when it's over.
Patience is key, there is no other.
Hardship and deeds. Still beautiful adventure.
Torch been passed, since first ancestor.

Younger, I thought my life would stop.
This idea, in my head, would often pop.
Your wisdom took time to be planted.
When you left, it made sense, blossomed.

It's the way you were embracing your flaws.
It's the way you gave me time, second chances.
Not wanting a clone, but a sovereign version.
You helped the closest and a random person.

Don't mind me, sometimes I speak in the past,
Talking about when I made you breakfast.
I won't haunt you, I'll let you rest.
Let's talk in what you find interest.

No more celebrations with you ever.
Really no need, I downloaded you deeper.
You'll be where I will be, forever.
Our connection will only get better.

How would I have known Love at its purest?
Thankful. He put in my life the best.
I might be right. I might be biased.
Who cares at this point? I just feel blessed.

I need to stay here for Now,
Until it has been decided otherwise,
To do like you and finish my part.
Deserve the best of the other side.

No need to be famous, nor conquer immortality.
Just gain one loyal heart, for eternity.
That's the real definition of posterity,
What I hold precious, sacred legacy.

Oil painting on canvas, illustrating the path into
an old mystical wood.

In the Wood

Magical Wood, Beautiful Hood.
Enchanting path, through my reptilian
mood.
As I go deep inside, the magical wood,
My ancestor-fears appear in the hood.

Uncertain, frightened, fearful of Nature,
I forgot that Humans have become mature.
I hear whispers. You're the king Now!
Your skin is thick, to you creation bow. . .

"Dust off History, your past aura.
Humans walked, into a new Era,"
Said the trees, keepers of Akashic memories.
Maybe they're real, or illusory dreams.

Tell me my secrets! Even the weirds . . .
I feel safe, opened are my ears.
Show me my powers, and my flaws.
Why do I still stick to old false laws?

Truths, my mind thinks it perceives.
He never lived them, just believes.
In my heart though, they feel so real.

I am ready like never before.
Do not babysit me no more!
I am a grown girl, open the door.

I came in search, of a deeper state.
My soul do not accommodate.
Can't you see? that I am High.
Flying amongst, birds in the sky.

Trust me! the way I trust you, please.
Flood into my veins, with no ease.
What's missing here to encounter?
My last stage, and surrender . . .

How to return to what's less than free?
No more concerned, but more, happy
To find joy, in just being me.
Ain't that how it's supposed to be?

Day after day, I retrieve me.
Old Earth becomes a souvenir.
A chapter, in the book of History.
New Earth waits for me, and those
Who want old messages to close.

Spend days or years in your Avatar . . .
You haven't lived, until from your heart.

Poem 3

The Teacher

I found it better, to go there lonely . . .
  Then saw you do it, effortlessly . . .
So open, so light, you make it easy.
One snap! You connect, quickly.

Crystal clear, you embody it so fast.
I struggled to get the test, passed.
But with you, O, my Teacher.
I aim, I hit, my hands surrender.
Never miss, with you got better.

You unlock portals for those
Who want to join and win the cause.
Voices in my head say *Don't objectify*.
Your Master is a medium, not the "I".
"I get it. Don't worry," I reply.

Hear my words loud, I don't intend
To stay around more than is meant.
I sit at a distance, magical instant.

Closing eyes, breathing heavy.
Thoughts leave the house, soon my body
Grounded in that which is real me.
All the rest is appearance only.

Oil on wood, illustrating the first garden.

Poem 4

Remember

It all began, together in your Kingdom
    Made me from void, but not from random.
Used an essence, to make me blossom.
Breathed me into life, Mantra Om . . .
You said: "Go live, under the Dome,
Once Eden built, I'll let you come."

That day, you married in me the bodies
Within the vortex, spiraling energies . . .
Up to whomever wants to make it squeeze
Into perfection, be and it is!

Ordered to all, to perform a bow!
They had to speak, and say the vow,
In front of whom, you decided now,
Would govern Earth and wear the crown.

On this pinnacle, I felt dizzy.
Didn't believe, mind got crazy.
How could a fleshy deserve it all?
Be most darling, standing tall!
"Back off, back off," said the call . . .

My shadow then, came to my ears,
Whispered non-sense. What is it I hear?
Move away, separate, you're not his dear.
Can't you see, O Blinded? Your place not here.
Ego born, from that day, from first tear . . .

It went on: Man is no masterpiece.
Barely a solid. Greatness, dismiss!
For His care, and love, you'll have to bleed,
Sweat and sorrow, hard work and deed,
Lacking, always, he'll be in need.

Quickly, made me forget my mission,
Being an Angel? It's a better position.
Attain immortality? Make a decision!
Blinded, I could only hear an opinion.

Fading away . . . my true destiny . . .
When at my feet, Angels were on their knee.
In Eternity garden I was already.

Fooled I was, don't make fun of me.
It was the shock, friends, some empathy.
I followed the illusion of a false duty.
The illusion, of a better state, calling me.

But, when the veil was finally lifted,
And the mirage been dissipated,
My shadow and its sadness, dissolved,
And in the revealing flame, burned.

Peace came back, a reminder.
For it only serves, to remember
Your true Self, that nothing stains,
No need to act, not even be a Saint.

Even in Chaos, I can only be yours.
Your essence, in me, is all that pours.

To celebrate my return, The Cosmos dancing.
Circular movements, got me, trancing.
Chanting, singing, to the everlasting.
All that is, you made it existing!

Unconditional love, I am now, accepting . . .

Oil on canvas, sailing towards the Rock.

Poem 5

The Rock

I discovered splendor, on your face.
    Softness, spreading, all over the place.
Handsome, and O, Beautiful Look,
A wonder, when I open your book.
Grace, love, you got, and took.

Higher realms lie, behind your doors.
Portals, that you reveal, inverted mirrors.
In Life, this Ocean, tides come and go,
Wisdom, for others, you only show.

Waves of darkness, I see. Others of bliss.
Yet, your Presence feels like a kiss.
Closer to me than my breath,
I hold you, precious, in my chest.

Taught me to say what's best,
Or, to keep silent, 'cause you know,
When you Believe, and allow,
This is how, miracles flow . . .

Silent! Not only from talk.
Thoughts in your mind, do not walk.
To you, all seem transparent,
House of Glass, so apparent.

You never show, nor hide
The Ugly, nor sparkling side.
To your principles I abide.

Smile. Either, you're burdened, or High,
Temporary, has agenda, won't let you fly,
Stick with the Rock, stick with me,
I was, I am, and always will be free . . .

Oil on canvas, illustrating a dawn

Poem 6

Mind at Rest

I don't wanna use my mind, anymore!
    The day I found you, I found it all.
I am fine keeping knowledge about
How to cook, or, to find the South.
But beliefs and conclusions, I want to stop.

I tell myself every night before bed,
I am not me. I am the "I".

Angels come and visit through dreams,
Thoughts, people's tongues, and birds singing.
They tell me, you're still dual, just drop it.
It's all part of the game, accept it.

Wonder with joy, there is so much to discover!
Not only physics, but sketching a rover.
You're never away, even if cleaning a house.
All your moves are a meditation to us.

I know what they mean, I think?
But, I am longing for more, to sink.
Maybe dying before to die?
Ascending, reincarnating, before paradise.

Spirit Aura, shining on all surface,
No longer homesick, this is my place.
I am fine in being here and now
Where I am supposed to be all the time.

I experience each dimension—
One of music, one of equation.
Quench me in your vibration.

Downloading the virtual
Real life not just Conceptual.
Even in a shy smile I see
Beauty and love all around me.

Your quest? Your purpose?
Are right under your nose.

Poem 7

You Are Loved

You are loved.
Can't you see?

Before your morning shower
You shall receive my power.

Stop, chasing significance,
Stop, chasing me,
Approval, validation, are not your needs.
I am your blood, I am your cells' deeds.

How can you get closer to your breath?
Don't blame them, for only you can get
That you either block me, or, let me set.

See me clearly, in your bones
Go no more, searching for clones.

By the stars! And, by the Moon!
By the Sun that shines at noon!
I made you last, 'cause you're my best.

Where I want you
You'll always be.
Your sweat and hardship
Don't make me trip.

I am the richest, I have no need!
I made Man as my perfect breed.

End up the struggle,
Recognize your power,
Dare, and let me flower.

I'll swipe up your fears,
And transform your tears,
From sadness to cheer.
Let celebration appear!

Look not far, you already are
In the heart of my heart
'Cause I want you, as my avatar.

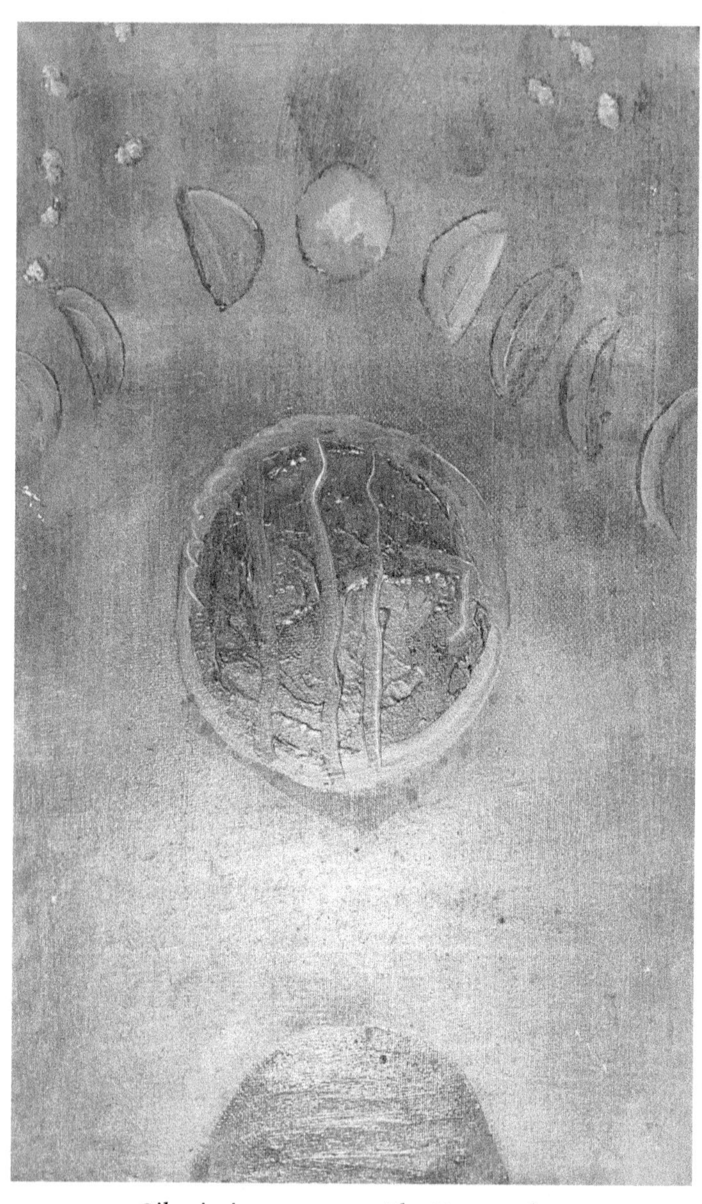

Oil painting on canvas, The Moon cycles.

Poem 8

The Moon

The moon is Happy
   The twelves are far.
No energies, touching
In void, just hiding

Who knows the cycles better than her?
She Knows when to speed, or to ponder.
To shine, to shut dark, both with pride,
All is important, relevant to her ride.

The Queen of Time, and gestation.
Wise guidance in each season.
She sets the clock, for what's next.
Teaches patience, in calculus text.

It's not against constancy
To change looks when coursing.
Always showing up is written in her book.
Doesn't mean she'll appear in the same look.

Some call her moody, others mystical.
Depends on your crystal ball,
Not to mention, consciousness level . . .

She is not common nor ordinary.
You'll get polished just by her proxy.
Everything she makes shiny.

Accused of making waves!
Oblivious to see, they fail.
Without her, Chaos will prevail.

Poem 9

Love Heritage

As I awaken, I now remember
Joy on our first encounter.
You gave me love unconditionally,
Always here to cuddle with me

Fantastic stories in my ears,
Fabulous tales and fairies,
Beautiful songs to make me sleep,
Morals I was too busy to keep

Memories of the day you told me:
"When you get conscious, I'll throw a party."
I smiled, knowing that I had access to
Your love, no matter what I do.

If hurt, your shoulders were my ease
To sooth me in and pain release.
Reassuring, smiling at my face.
O Dear, you're so hard to replace.

You give no judgement nor dismiss.
Life would take care of this.
Present, yet lighter than a leaf
Other behaviors are a belief.

But you were human, so you left.
So older, I dared, initiated myself,
Struggled to self-educate.
Slower than a turtle, moved ahead.

Not that I didn't try, or do my best;
It was just not happening.
That's how it was, I accepted it.
Maybe real Will, didn't show up yet.

Awareness waiting, in the corner near.
So a sad day, that lasted a year.
Here is what I could see in me, my dear:

Lost souls, with high potentials,
Wasting their Time in wrong credentials.
Wanderers, living hidden in misery,
Using Genius, on fake models, they copy.
Whilst "I", wants to shine in them, individually.

It calls them back, constantly, they see it:
As hardship striking on them, with no pity.
Help sent, for a second chance.
Each one, at his Will's pace.

Not mean, not bad nor devilish.
Just stupid, ignorant, still childish.
Missing the play in stupid adventures,
Thinking it's games, or lazy ventures.

I ventured to forgive everyone,
And I, myself, was number One
And recovered what lovers had
Left for me: the guided path.

Soft Pillars, they make a Cocoon House,
Warmth, and comfort flowing out
Here to deliver goodness and sweeties,
More than nurture, spoiling me always.

Billion graves full of important ones.
Still, you will often find those persons
who live in suspended gardens.
No good nor bad subsist,
Only life happenings exist.

They don't see you as an investment,
No pressure, no pushing. Flowing current.
Few years with them charge you fully,
Fill your emotions up for eternity.

Passing tourists who forever live,
Visitors, that come, give, and leave.
Forever imprinted in you, their image is
Fondness, honey, and sweeties.

Capricious, inconstant, silly you can
Freely be when around them.

Catapulted where in vain I could not reach.
That night I discovered what they did preach.
For the first one slept happy, speechless.
I became acquainted with the awareness
that until then I never experienced.

She hugged me and I cried loud:
"Where have you been hanging out?
Lovers died before you showed up!"

She smiled but accused me of being busy,
Then went on, "They are fine, don't worry.
Seeing you now made them happy."

Things have happened since that day,
Wonders, fabulous, I must say.

Acrylic painting on canvas.

Poem 10

Astral Vision

So, in my bed, I slipped that night.
Beyond, I came, to join your knights.
Finally deserved, to visit the other side.
Closed my eyes, other senses opened wide.

Feeling to thought, always precedes
Primary cause, after-life realms.

Before my eyes, my soul escaped,
And in the skies, was thrown away.
Delivered from the weight of my body.
No more beliefs, nor thoughts of tyranny.
Lighter she felt, parallel reality.

Feather sucked, into their domain,
A place that Ego could not attain.
Beyond the spheres' circumference
In what seemed like heaven's preference.

We were one, in a misty cloud.
In circle, Angels repeated loud:
"You are and you are existence,
Mind and matter transcendence."

Their freshly time spent in apotheosis,
Drinking your words and your actions,
Even if experiencing you without veils,
Even if closer to you than anything.

Oh, not incarnated, they were chanting,
Their amazing love, every day growing,
When You they were already adoring.

How lucky, to own an elastic heart
That's blown with bliss, infinite space.

You said, "Go. Don't get jealous.
All, even they, are at your service.
Be more patient; you will see this."

I went back in, pulled by my waiting purpose.
Nothing in me erased, I still remember.
I kept my shape, still something different,
Like an illusion that I had clung to too much,
Like a tan that lasted more than summer.
All I had to do was to dust it.

How to continue ignoring the Sun?
Bright, still soft, wanting you to wake up.

Poem 11

Self-Talk

Today I don't wanna do anything.
    The world is just fine without me.
But I don't wanna be silent either.
I'll come to love, I'll vibrate higher.

Not even coming, I'm here already,
Snuggled up in you, arms around me.
My heart is like a cloud.
Nothing stays in me.
Spongeous, made of praise
And beautiful daisies.
Everything else, just passing.

Bathing in this air ether,
Benevolence, warm ardor,
Infinite current flowing
Without end nor beginning.

I hear a voice saying, "Come back to reality.
You've still got Things to accomplish.
This is not where you're meant to live,
Not yet; work is still waiting.

I smile and say to my Self,
"Nothing truer than the Self.
How to access this nest
If not go into it to rest?"

Today, 'cause tomorrow
I do not yet know.
I may be, and I may not.

I gaze back to the Origins,
Then glance to far futures.
The same vision, Time offers:

"We are one in your garden,
Long before it all started
And when it is all over.

I follow my guidance, answer my call.
The signs abound, around the All
Through this inverted mirror that they call reality.
Each time I dare taking a step, a way is revealed.

Follow my lamp, carry it, you say.
I'll make it shine in every place.
Meditate, observe, feel me, yes,
With love, truth, and beauty.
Only rest on me, you have said,
Because I am the Only.
Connect with me by knowing yourself.

In the meantime, I can but not much
Forget that these two places
Are my home ad vitam aeternam.

Revelare

You only appear when I cease to resist.
Before I met you, I was sure you exist.
Took me a lifetime, you're not easy to reach.
So many times, I was about to quit.
Well, even this thought could not persist.

How could it have been otherwise?
Bigger than an imagination used wide.
What Am I, if not your better ferment?
I feel your love in all inches of my flesh.
My "I" and your "I" are one now.

I want to erase myself and let you in forever.
I saw you in people's eyes when they looked to a Lover.
Some embodied you for hours.
Others grabbed and let you flower.

At that moment I heard your whispers
In the winds through the branches,
In the song of the birds,
In the music of the rains,
In falls running through the rivers.

pottery tile, illustrating a mountain village.

Poem 13

I Know

I know I'm not doing anything.
　　Not that I don't intend to,
But it's all "a" happening.
Impatient, I wake up every day
Then quickly realize: *What to do anyway?*

In an already perfect deployment?
In such an orderly existence?
Destroy? Create? Or transform?
Rise the Sun? Or set it?

I don't do anything, I know.
I sense though, that through me you draw.
You take my fellows' hands and mine,
To fill up space, with manmade crafts.

We mark this Earth that never lies.
Traces, tracks and timelines,
Stubborn, always keeping records
Of Human mastery evolutions.

Left for those provided with Reason,
To turn backward just to reckon:

All die, but some petrified.
No accident, it was intended
To leave signs on our path.
So, we study to understand
How it all started. Got unfolded.

Hands shaking in muds, tongues confused by brains,
Trying in vain to sculpt in the clay.
The image sent by Spirit from within.

We get down to business.
Some spend their lives there.
Others quickly understand that
The original will never take shape.

Your creation and ours are one,
An equation, a painting or a poem.
But isn't that what you wanted for us?

A force that moves everything and pulls us
Because nothing ever stands still,
Not even the smallest sand grain.
Everything lives, bubbling so fast.

We start again, believe it's fresh creation
When all is about accumulation.
Yes, we are our ancestors' heirs,
Fruits of all their seeds and plants.

We view your creation as perfect,
And maybe this is how you see ours.
Clay, in nimble though fragile hands.

We continue, and we dare to look at the sky.
What is your point? Where are you taking me? Is there
an end?

To this Force which is Yours, O Only One,
Appears your Will in the good and in the rest.
I beg you to use me only for what is best.

Angels come to me and say,
"You don't seem to want it so much."
I get angry, and proclaim,
"I will bleed my way there."

They smile, leaving me perplexed.
"This is not how you'll get things done.
Learn more, you need to grow."

I take it back, the sword was not given to me
And I didn't ask for it either.
When I finally calm down, I see
That the key is not to force it.

It is by moving, that open before us
The gates of eternity and ascension.

You Are Not an Object to Find

At first you came to me in the form of others.
You fed me, tucked me in, taught me words.
I sew threads all over us.

Sucked you in me, no place for air,
Breathing you, till we suffocated.
Mimicking you, to become you.

Sculptures were freer to move.
It lasted years, almost forever,
Until the day I realized you weren't they.

Then you appeared in his form.
You were kind and handsome,
You treated me with respect.

I sew threads all over us.
Sucked you in, eyes could see the beauty outside.
No more discoveries, no more wonders.

Breathed same air, till we suffocated,
Until the day I realized you weren't he.

Then you appeared in the form of success.
Shining gold, bling-bling rocks,
Wild cars, silky dress codes.

Material beauty, earthly attachment
Defining us in what couldn't last,
Until the day it told me—"I need space."

My job is to circulate,
Not to be trapped with you; it's toxic.
It left, and I realized it wasn't you.

Finally, you approached me in the form of a guide.
You taught me relevance, clarified
This is when I got closest to you.

You were there at my fingertips I almost caught you,
Until the day you left without looking back.

Because they were looking for you too.
At least I knew you weren't an object.

All my life I've looked for you in a face, in an object,
In beauty, love, or instant pleasures.
Stolen moments that never lasted.
To them, blinded, I was kept attached.

All change or fade but you are not they.

So, I gave up my quest to find the highest.
I accepted, sadly, but then felt calmest
That you weren't from this world.

Futile quest, useless race, I dared
This time intimately asking you to show yourself.

Not that you were a ghost.
Just wanted to communicate.
You started my cleanse, emptied me to set.
I then experienced you and you never left.

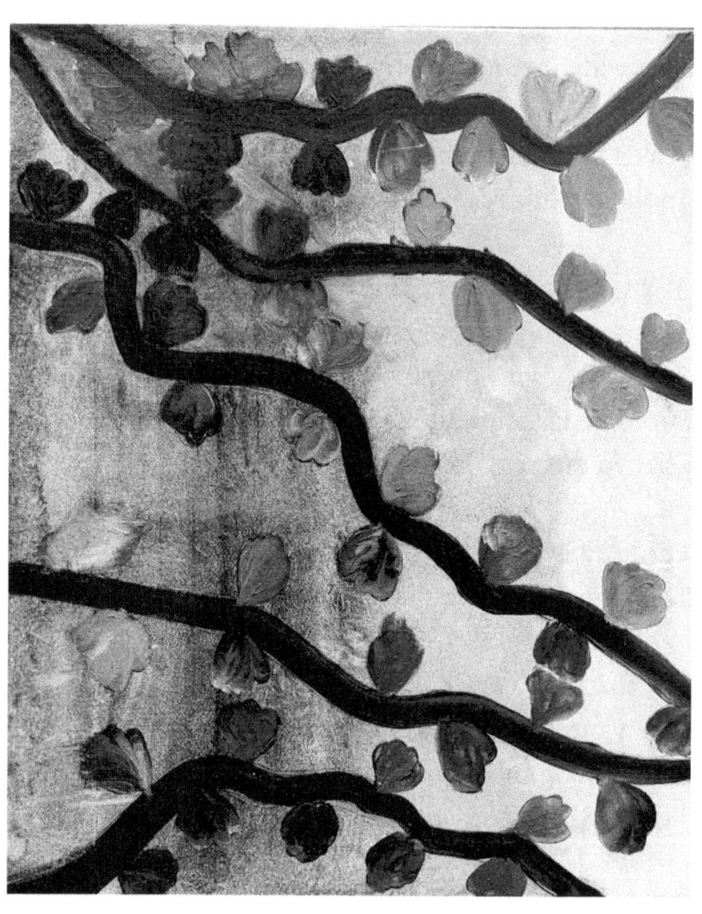

oil on canvas.

Time Distortion

Tick after tick, again and again,
  Tick and ticking, until glitching.

A bird passes in the Sky,
Makes the whole matrix fall apart.
A Sun shining through a cloud
Opens before you magical portals.

Time, Swag, sharp, precise, still there is
A fast tracking, no cheating, just sneak in
Other planes and fantastic journeys,
The harder to master, yet most rewarding.

When One abides to Earthly time,
He ascends to vertical relative height.
Dizzy, too fast, too much at first.
But before long, you'll like the taste.

People ask, what superpower I would like.
I know it's time that I want to ride.
Gestation, dating, chronology ,
Lines, cycles, and more geometry.

Yes, stellar objects shine beauty,
But there is more to it.
A cosmic clock, with clear trajectory.
Still, I negotiate hidden trail ways.

Change timeline, you change sight.
Twelve and sixes add up, make nine.
It's contradictory, seen from 3D.
Becoming naïve can be the key.

A wild horse that you end up riding,
Not by force but more by trusting.

T for time, and T for thinking.
Ain't fun, that's all there is to it.
T for Time and T for traveling.
How would space modulate without Time allowing?

Resistance creates Time gap
And at times receiving what's best to get.

A machine? No need! I can go back
Or speed, Time lapsing 5D.
Why to burden with heavily objects?
Time is a blessing, a first draw test.

Reward or forward, a stromatolite,
Silent from talk, at least doesn't lie.

Permits to check or dismiss unwanted.
It's not your first try when you do it,
But when you are thinking about it.

"Me" can be prisoner of my body,
But my mind wanders with liberty.
Going to the past makes it the Future,
And now the present becomes my ancestor.

They've been warning me: know these rules.
No one has the luxury to ignore the rules
Of how things were made working.

Time is capricious.
Don't provoke nor try to control it.
Understand it exists, it wants to manifest.
Leave a place for it and he'll be your friend.

flowers painting.

Poem 16

Figuring You Out

I haven't figured you out,
   Yet, I sit at my window in « Aha »
Admiring your clouds in the sky.
Lose track of time, reading your stars.

Then remember it is all equal.
Earthly is just as beautiful as celestial.
Above looks at below in « Wow! »
Knowing it's all One. But how?

Torturing my mind to get you can be fatal.
Instead, I enjoy your creation, feels special.
All is permanent, only you are eternal.
Your love around us, circular.

I haven't figured you out . . .
All day, it's you I am thinking about.
Spent decades in Love and bow.
You're my shelter and my house . . .

Instructions for using AR

LET AUGMENTED REALITY CHANGE HOW YOU READ A BOOK

With your smartphone, iPad or tablet you can use the  **Hasmark AR** app to invoke the augmented reality experience to literally read outside the book.

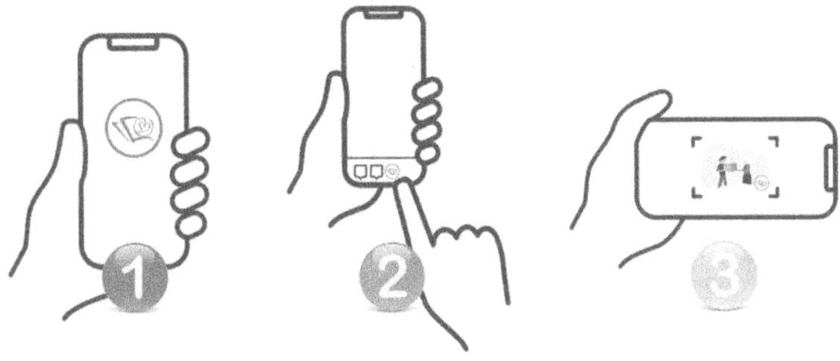

1. Download the **Hasmark app** from the **Apple App Store** or **Google Play**

2. Open and select the (vue) option

3. Point your lens at the full image with the and enjoy the augmented reality experience.

Go ahead and try it right now with the Hasmark Publishing International logo.

About The Author

$\mathcal{M}$ouna SAQUAQUE has always lived with the echo of existential questions: Who am I? Where am I? Why am I here? Is there a purpose to existence? But most importantly why do I believe Happiness is my birthright?

When she finally embarked in answering those questions, she started sharing her understandings by translating them into writings and meditations on life from a Human perspective.

She used to believe, and now knows, that the most important experience to install in one's life is Peace of Mind.

Finding the balance between making things happen and letting things happen. A game of cooperation between life unfolding and Human's expressions of existence, where self-knowledge is key.

Visit the author's website:
www.mounasaquaque.com

More books:

"Who am I? Where am I?"
https://www.amazon.com/dp/1989756255

From: Circe'

To: Kids who love to write stories!

How would you like to have your story in a book? A real book!
Hearts to be Heard will make that happen.

Get started now at
HeartstobeHeard.com

Also visit HH Kid's Corner for creative writing activities!
HeartstobeHeard.com/kids-corner/